THE
SABBATH

DAYAN DR. I. GRUNFELD

THE

SABBATH

a guide to its understanding
and observance

FOURTH, RESET EDITION

FELDHEIM PUBLISHERS
Jerusalem / New York

First published 1954
Second edition 1956
Third edition 1959
Fourth, reset edition 1981
Reprint 1988
Hardcover edition ISBN 0-87306-266-3
Paperback edition ISBN 0-87306-272-8

Phototypeset at the Feldheim Press

Philipp Feldheim Inc.

Printed in Israel

In Memoriam

Since the last edition of this book appeared, Dayan Grunfeld, ז״ל, has passed on to his eternal reward, and a few words on his life and work would certainly be appropriate here.

Dayan Isidor Grunfeld (1900-1975) — lawyer, Dayan of the Court of the Chief Rabbi, communal leader, educator and prolific writer — was above all an ardent follower of Rabbi Samson Raphael Hirsch. His whole life was dedicated to interpreting the ideas and works of the Master and making them accessible to our generation. He was an eloquent advocate for the application of the Hirschian approach to solving the problems of living in the 20th century.

From Hirsch he inherited his breadth of vision. He was keenly aware of the currents of thought in the secular world and welcomed every opportunity to demonstrate the relevance of Torah to the wider problems of mankind. How he fought against the narrow mentality which sees Torah as the possession and interest of only a small and isolated group of people! It says much for the man, however, that he remained on the best of terms with those very circles and gained their admiration, affection and respect.

This little book, in which the present writer had the privilege of collaborating, was the *bikkurim* — the first fruit — of his extensive literary activity. It has been called "the finest exposition of the Sabbath available in English" and has been translated into several languages, though strangely enough a Hebrew edition still awaits publication.

The book is unique among expositions of the Sabbath in that it sets out to show the significance of the halachic Sabbath and to demonstrate that abstention from *melakhah*, in all its ramifications, is the living heart and core of Sabbath observance. This is the aspect of the Jewish Sabbath so often decried by the ignorant as "senseless concentration on trivial details." Insightfully Rabbi Hirsch promulgated a majestic concept of *issur melakhah* as abstention for one day in seven from all creative activity, thus bearing eloquent testimony to the need to live in God's world as His creatures and to use all our human powers in His service. This concept, so well presented in this book, must once and for all put an end to such unfortunate misunderstandings. And no one who has read this book will ever again be able honestly to use the outworn argument that the Sabbath law against kindling fire applied only to times when making a fire involved the hard labor of knocking two heavy stones together (see p. 56).

The quarter-century that has passed since the book's first appearance, which has witnessed the increasing de-humanization and de-personalization of man and the world-wide erosion of moral standards, has served only to re-inforce the message to which Dayan Grunfeld was so passionately committed—the eternal relevance of the laws of the Torah and particularly those of the Sabbath, to the spiritual regeneration of the Jewish people and of all mankind.

A.C.

Jerusalem
Kislev 5741/1981

Preface to the Third Edition

The second edition of *The Sabbath*, which was published in 5716 (1956), has been unobtainable for some time. I have therefore gladly acceded to the suggestion of the publishing firm of Philipp Feldheim, Inc. of New York, to publish an American edition of this work. (The first two editions were published by the Sabbath League of Great Britain.)

This third edition is an almost unaltered reprint of the second. The wide circulation of this book among English-reading Jews is a welcome proof of the fact that our people continue to see in the observance of the Sabbath the secret of Israel's survival.

I would like to express my gratitude to the publishers for the loving care they have taken in the preparation of this edition.

London   I.G.
Tishri 5720/1959

Preface to the Second Edition

The friendly reception which the first edition of this publication has received, especially in the United States, has been a source of great satisfaction to me. The fact that the first edition was sold out in little more than a year, shows that there is need for this book, which is being used by private individuals, schools and study groups all over the world. Unfortunately, illness prevented me from attending earlier to the issue of this second edition.

In the preface to the first edition, I expressed my gratitude to Rabbi Aryeh Carmell, for his help in preparing this publication. He has since greatly added to my indebtedness to him by supervising the distribution of this book. That it is obtainable at such a low price is largely due to the fact that the work usually done by publishers was carried out by Rabbi Carmell in his capacity as Hon. Secretary to the Sabbath League of Great Britain.

The second edition is an almost unaltered reprint of the first. The index, however, has been enlarged, following the friendly advice of reviewers and readers, and thanks are due to Mrs. Cassie Cooper, who kindly undertook this task.

Menachem Av 5716   I.G.

Preface

This little volume has mainly a practical purpose: to be a guide to the proper understanding and observance of the Sabbath, the foundation of our faith. Although the book is small in size, much time, work and thought have been spent on it.

At the outset I would like to express my deep gratitude to Rabbi Aryeh Carmell who has helped me throughout the preparation and publication of this book and has contributed various sections to it.

Any presentation of the Sabbath as the fundamental institution of Judaism must of necessity fall into two parts: an aggadic one, dealing with the underlying ideas of Sabbath, and a halachic one, explaining the laws of its practical observance. I have tried to blend the one with the other.

For the aggadic part I have mostly drawn on the *aggadah* of Tractate *Shabbath* in the Babylonian Talmud; on the Midrashic literature; and among modern works, particularly on the writings of Rabbi Samson Raphael Hirsch, one of the outstanding Jewish thinkers of the last century. On the halachic side, apart from the standard codes and works on Jewish Law,(רמב״ם, שלחן ערוך, חיי אדם, כלכלת שבת), I have made use of Rabbi E. Biberfeld's *Sabbath-Vorschriften*, which was published in Germany some fifty years ago and proved very popular. My thanks are due to Mrs. Fanny Kahn, who put her translation of that little book at my disposal.

I am also grateful to Dayan A. Rapoport and Rabbi Dr.

S. Mannes for their assistance in connection with the halachic part of this publication.

Thanks are due, as well, to Norman Solomons Esq., M.A., for many helpful suggestions.

I venture to hope that this book will deepen the understanding of our holy Sabbath, serve as an introduction to the knowledge of its laws, and eventually lead the reader to the study of its halachic and aggadic sources. I trust further that it will be helpful to Jewish educators. Finally, I pray that, with the help of God, this book will assist those who unfortunately have lost the Sabbath, to regain the peace and blessing which are to be found in its observance.

London   I.G.
5714/1954

☙ contents ☙

1

THE SPIRIT OF SABBATH

2

THE CONCEPT OF *MELAKHAH*

3

SABBATH OBSERVANCE
IN PRACTICE

4

THE CELEBRATION OF SABBATH

5

SABBATH IN THE MODERN WORLD

The train dragged on with its human freight. Pressed together like cattle in the crowded trucks, the unfortunate occupants were unable even to move. The atmosphere was stifling. As the Friday afternoon wore on, the Jewish men and women in the Nazi transport sank deeper and deeper into their misery.

Suddenly an old Jewish woman managed with a great effort to move and open her bundle. Laboriously she drew out — two candlesticks and two challoth. *She had just prepared them for Sabbath when she was dragged from her home that morning. They were the only things she had thought worth while taking with her. Soon the Sabbath candles lit up the faces of the tortured Jews and the song of* Lekhah Dodi *transformed the scene. Sabbath with its atmosphere of peace had descended upon them all.*

This story, reported to the author by an eyewitness who escaped, is by no means an isolated one in our long history. Countless similar episodes could be cited of Jews who clung to Sabbath in the face of death and in spite of death. What is the secret of Sabbath's hold over the Jewish heart? Mere sentiment will not account for it. Perhaps, consciously or unconsciously, it is a realization of the ancient word:

> *"Between Me and the children of Israel it is a sign for ever . . ."* (Exodus 31:17)

For Sabbath expresses all the innermost longings of the Jewish soul, and each of its many facets reflects something of the Divine radiance.

I have a precious gift in my treasury, said God to Moses: "Sabbath" is its name; go and tell Israel I wish to present it to them (*Shabbath* 10b).

The Spirit of Sabbath

1 *The Meaning of the Sabbath*

Our Sages call the Sabbath *yesod ha'emunah*, the very foundation of our faith. This is no exaggeration. For the loftiest thoughts by which Judaism has ennobled the human mind, the highest ideals for which our people have been striving for thousands of years at the cost of innumerable lives, all are centered in the Sabbath.

DIGNITY OF WORK

"Six days shall you labor and do all your work." The basis of the Sabbath is thus work — labor dignified by God's commandment. Work is not a degradation but man's holy birthright. How many centuries, millennia even, did it take the world to grasp this fundamental truth! It is a long way indeed from the Greek and Roman conception of labor as degrading, with the resultant lack of rights of the laborer, to the present-day status of the working man. How much social unrest and misery, how many wars and revolutions, how much bloodshed could mankind have been spared, had the Biblical ideal of the dignity of labor been made from the very beginning the basis of the social order!

Jewish tradition tells us that Adam became reconciled to his fate only when he was told that he would have to work. Work is indeed the prerogative of free-born creative man. "Great is work," our Sages say, "for it honors him who does it."[1]

SPIRITUAL FREEDOM

Yet work is not all. Work can make man free, but one can also be a slave to work. When God created heaven and earth, says the Talmud, they went on unreeling endlessly, "like two bobbins of thread," until their Creator called out to them "Enough!"[2] God's creative activity was followed by the Sabbath, when He deliberately ceased from His creative work. This, more than anything, shows Him to us as the free Creator freely controlling and limiting the creation He brought into being according to His will — the Creator with a purpose.

It is thus not "work," but "ceasing from work" which God chose as the sign of His free creation of the world. By ceasing from work every Sabbath, in the manner prescribed by the Torah, the Jew bears witness to the creative power of God. He also reveals

1. Babylonian Talmud: *Nedarim*, 49b.
2. Ibid., *Chagigah*, 12a.

Man's true greatness. The stars and the planets, having once started on their eternal rounds, go on blindly, ceaselessly, driven by nature's law of cause and effect. Man, however, by an act of faith, can put a limit to his labor, so that it will not degenerate into purposeless drudgery. By keeping Sabbath the Jew becomes, as our Sages say, *domeh l'yotzero* — "like God Himself." He is, like God, work's master, not its slave.

Man is truly great, however, only if he willingly cooperates in God's plan for the world, making use of his freedom to serve God and his fellow-men. Then he becomes, as the Sages put it, "a partner in the work of creation."[3] Yet man's very freedom can lead to his downfall. His great powers over the world of nature, which enable him to control and master it, harness its energies, mold and adapt it to his will — these very powers make it fatally easy for man to think of himself in the guise of creator, responsible to no one higher than himself. We of the twentieth century have seen what happens to the world and to mankind when such ideas prevail.

But here Sabbath comes to the rescue. As we shall see later in greater detail, we have here perhaps the most fundamental aspect of Sabbath observance.

It is possible to recognize the basic truth of God's creation of the world. But what does this mean to the average man and woman? Very little indeed. But here, as always, the Torah is not satisfied with mere theory. The Torah is interested in deeds — the

3. Babylonian Talmud: *Shabbath* 10a.

practical outcome. Put like this the doctrine comes to life: "Living in God's world as His creatures, we must use all our human powers in His service." Only thus can we justify our existence, and at the same time ensure our own welfare and that of the human race.

The unique provisions of the Sabbath law serve to keep this very practical consideration in the forefront of our minds. We are stopped on this one day from exercising our characteristic human powers of producing and creating in the material world. By this very inactivity we lay these powers in homage at the feet of God Who gave them. This basic Sabbath-idea will be developed more fully in later chapters. If we strain our ears, however, we may even now catch what the Sabbath is trying to say to us.

In fact, it says to us every week what God told the first human being:

"I have placed you in this world of mine; everything I have created is for you. Set your mind to it that you do not corrupt and destroy my world."

Here we have the essence of Sabbath. The same act that proclaims man's freedom also declares his subservience to God. To use all one's powers in the service of God — there is no greater freedom than this.

2 Sabbath and Life

Another blessing flows from Sabbath — the blessing of *menuchah* — "rest." This *menuchah* is something much more than physical rest. It is an attitude of mind, a spiritual state, induced by the experience that is Sabbath. It is compounded of many things.

There is the joy at being released from bondage to the pressing demands of everyday life.

Quite apart from the bondage of work, there are the insistent demands of our mechanical civilization—the bus, the car, the telephone; the demands, too, of our mechanical entertainment industry—radio, television, the cinema. . . . Until we reflect, most of us are unaware of the toll which these things take of our vital energy; we do not realize the extent of our enslavement. To take only one example: how many of us can sit alone in a room together with a ringing telephone without answering it? The summons is irresistible: we know that sooner or later we *must* answer it. On Sabbath this "must" does not exist. The relaxation, the relief of spirit, which a real Jewish Sabbath brings must be experienced to be believed.

The spirit of *menuchah* finds its positive expression in the Sabbath meals in which the happy companionship of family and friends, the enjoyment of good food, the table-songs in praise of God and the Sabbath, all combine to form an entirely unique experience.

In this Sabbath atmosphere it is easy to feel the nearness of God, and to face life without worry and without regrets, in the confidence that we are all in His care.

With body refreshed and nervous tension relaxed, the mind is stimulated in its turn to achieve closer contact with God by the study of His Torah, not as an intellectual pastime, but in the full knowledge that it is the only source of truth and true living for the Jew. If we make this spiritual activity the positive content of the Sabbath's leisure hours, then when Sabbath goes out it will leave us in all respects better equipped for the tasks of the coming week — better equipped, in fact, for the task of living.

The blessings of Sabbath are not confined to the life of the individual.. After helping the Jew to find himself, Sabbath helps him to find his fellow-man. One of the basic motives given in the Torah for the Sabbath commandment is:

> "...that your manservant and maidservant may rest as well as you." (Deuteronomy 5:14)

The master like the servant — the servant like the master! Can anyone realize today what this equalization must have meant at a time when a bondservant was nothing but his master's animated tool, to be broken and destroyed at will? On the Sabbath servant and master meet as equals, as free human personalities. Sabbath restored to the slave his human dignity. Sabbath-rest and Sabbath-freedom applied also to the "stranger within the gates." Thus the foundation was laid for the brotherhood of man. Indeed, as we shall see, even the cattle are not excluded from the heavenly blessing of Sabbath-rest. Not even the animal may be denied the dignity due a creature of God.

Sabbath is thus a weekly-recurring divine protest against slavery and oppression. Lifting up his *kiddush* cup on Friday night, the Jew links the creation of the world with man's freedom, so declaring slavery and oppression deadly sins against the very foundation of the universe. Can one be surprised that tyrants of all times would not permit Israel to celebrate the Sabbath?

SPIRITUAL ASPIRATIONS

We have seen that Sabbath is the root of all spiritual and social progress, that it is connected with the highest thoughts and aspirations of man: God, the dignity of the human soul, the freedom and equality of man, the supremacy of spirit over matter. Small wonder, then, that the prophets of Israel took the Sabbath as the symbol of everything that is morally good and noble.

> "Happy is the man who does this, and the son of man who holds fast by it: who keeps the Sabbath from profaning it—and keeps his hand from doing any evil." (Isaiah 56:2)

The same idea of identifying the Sabbath with man's highest aspirations on earth is expressed in Nehemiah (9:13):

> "You came down also upon Mount Sinai and spoke with them from heaven and gave them right judgments and true laws, good statutes and commandments—and you made known unto them your holy Sabbath."

Our Sages with their unique gift for epigram gave expression to the fact that the Sabbath contains the sum and substance of Jewish life and thought in the words: "If God had not brought us to Mount Sinai and had only given us the Sabbath it would have been enough."[4] It would indeed have been enough, for Sabbath epitomizes the whole of Judaism.

4. Haggadah of Pesach.

The Concept of Melakhah

1 *What Is Melakhah?*

How is the Sabbath to be observed to ensure that its sublime purpose may be realized in the Jewish soul?

The Torah's answer is unmistakable. As we have seen, it is by refraining from work; the very word *shabbath* (in Hebrew) means just this.

"You shall do no manner of work..."

Again and again the Torah insists on this as the first condition, the center and essence of Sabbath observance.

We have now to consider exactly what the Torah means by "work" in this connection—and here we may be led to some rather unexpected conclusions.

MELAKHAH AND WORK

It is clear that "work" or, to use the Torah's own term, *melakhah*, is by no means identical with physical strain or exertion. This is shown by the simple legal fact that you are not a Sabbath-breaker if you carry a very heavy load inside your house, but if you carry even a small book from your house into the street you would be profaning the Sabbath. Nor is it true to say that what the Torah forbids is merely the carrying on of our everyday occupations. The Sabbath laws include this, but they include far more besides, and it is clear that they must be based on some different principle.

What is really meant by "work" in the Biblical injunction "You shall do no manner of work" can be ascertained only by careful study of the oral tradition. And it is best not to use the confusing translation "work" or "labor" but to keep to the technical term *melakhah*. A clear appreciation of the nature of *melakhah* is vitally important for the true understanding of Sabbath as the Torah itself means it to be observed, and as it is in fact observed to this day by those Jews mindful of their great heritage.

SABBATH IN THE TORAH

The main source in the Torah for the definition of *melakhah* is the command that all the various activities necessary for the construction of the Sanctuary in the desert should cease on Sabbath (Exodus 31:13). All these are thus expressly included in the term *melakhah*.

Here is a list of these activities, taken from the Mishnah (*Shabbath* 7:2):

1. Ploughing	4. Sheaf-making
2. Sowing	5. Threshing
3. Reaping	6. Winnowing

7. Selecting	22. Untying a knot
8. Sifting	23. Sewing
9. Grinding	24. Tearing
10. Kneading	25. Trapping
11. Baking	or hunting
12. Sheep-shearing	26. Slaughtering
13. Bleaching	27. Skinning
14. Combing	28. Tanning
raw materials	29. Scraping pelts
15. Dyeing	30. Marking out
16. Spinning	31. Cutting to shape
17, 18, 19.	32. Writing
Weaving	33. Erasing
operations	34. Building
20. Separating	35. Demolishing
into threads	36. Kindling a fire
21. Tying a knot	37. Extinguishing

38. The final hammer-blow (putting the finishing touch to a newly manufactured article)
39. Carrying from the private to the public domain (and vice versa)

If we examine this list, we discover a surprising fact. They are seen to form a cross-section of all the main types of human productive activity. This can hardly be accidental. However, it is not to our purpose now to inquire into possible reasons for this so far as the building of the Sanctuary is concerned. What does concern us is that the Torah has given us here a clear indication of the nature and scope of *melakhah*. In addition, certain types of *melakhah* are mentioned independently in the Torah, such as "carrying"

(Exodus 16:29; Numbers 15:32), and "lighting fire" (Exodus 35:3), and in each case important light is shed on the Sabbath law as a whole.

CENTRAL CONCEPT

The written law thus gives the outline of the Sabbath legislation. The oral tradition has only to fill in the details, by defining terms, and by applying the given principles to all the practical questions which arise in everyday life.

For all practical purposes, therefore, recourse must be had to the oral tradition — the *halakhah*.

Every student of the *halakhah* can see for himself the vast, logically constructed system of the Sabbath laws. The more deeply he studies, the more it will be borne in on him that it is indeed a system — not a haphazard mass of laws, but a consistent, co-ordinated body of legislation, derived from and conforming to one central, underlying idea.

What then is this unifying principle which underlies the concept of *melakhah*, and so forms the basis of the whole institution of Sabbath?

It is of the utmost importance to find such a general principle, for nothing has done so much harm to the proper observance of the Sabbath as the gross misconception that *melakhah* can be equated merely with physical effort or labor.

Many Jewish thinkers have tried to formulate a central concept of this sort, and so find the key to the whole vast system of the Sabbath laws. The exposition given by Rabbi Samson Raphael Hirsch, one of the foremost Jewish thinkers of the last century, is a most helpful one for the modern mind.

2 *The Idea Behind Melakhah*

In arriving at his interpretation of *melakhah*, Rabbi Samson Raphael Hirsch starts with the basic idea that the Sabbath testifies to God as the supreme Creator of heaven and earth and all they contain. Man, however, is engaged in a constant struggle to gain mastery over God's creation, to bring nature under his control. By the use of his God-given intelligence, skill and energy, he has in large measure succeeded in this. He is thus constantly in danger of forgetting his own creaturehood — his utter and complete dependence on the Lord of all things. He tends to forget that the very powers he uses in his conquest of nature are derived from his Creator, in whose service his life and work should be conducted.

ISRAEL'S TASK

In a world increasingly forgetful of God, Israel was entrusted with the task of preserving this all-important truth for the future salvation of all mankind. God willed therefore that the Jew, while subduing and controlling his environment like every other human being, must recognize, *and show that he recognizes*, that his powers are derived from One higher than himself. This recognition he is to express by dedicating one day in every week to God, and by refraining on this day from every activity which signifies human power over nature.

RENOUNCING MASTERY

On this day we renounce every exercise of intelligent, purposeful control over natural objects and forces, we cease from every act of human power, in order to proclaim God as the Source of all power. By refraining from human creating, the Jew pays silent homage to the Creator.

The essential characteristic of human creativeness is the intelligent purpose which directs it. This, then, is the import of the fundamental halachic principle which forms the basis of the whole of the Sabbath law: *Melekheth machasheveth aserah Torah*; i.e., "the Torah forbids as *melakhah* the realization of an intelligent purpose by practical skill."[1]

This, too, is the meaning of the principle, (otherwise obscure) which states that any act of pure destruction, however strenuous, is not a *melakhah* — כל המקלקלים פטורים.[2] Thus if one were to knock down a house simply with the idea of destroying it, one would not be doing a *melakhah* (although this would hardly be a recommended way of spending Sabbath, and the act would in any case be prohibited under the rabbinical safeguarding legislation; see below, Chapter 3). If however one were to do precisely the same act with the constructive purpose of clearing the site for rebuilding, one's act would be a *melakhah*.

We see clearly that it is the purpose that counts, and the *melakhah*-act can only be an expression of

---

1. Babylonian Talmud: *Sanhedrin*, 62b.
2. Ibid., *Shabbath*, 106a.

human creative intelligence if that purpose is constructive.

Melakhah thus includes within its scope any activity of a constructive nature which makes some significant change in our material environment — significant, that is, in relation to its usefulness for human purposes. Any act, however small, which demonstrates man's mastery of nature in this way is a *melakhah*, be it striking a light or washing clothes, tying a knot or building a house.

We have thus arrived at the definition we have been searching for. A *melakhah* is:

> an act that shows man's mastery over the world by the constructive exercise of his intelligence and skill.

ELOQUENT RESTRAINT

In the light of this exposition one can easily see how senseless is the oft-repeated argument that it is no exertion to switch on an electric light, or to write a word. As if the using of electricity were any less a conquest of nature because it happens to be effortless! Or as if writing a word were any less a manifestation of man's creative power because it seems so simple!

Actions can be more eloquent than words. By his complete renunciation of this type of activity on this day, the Jew, as the representative of mankind before God, solemnly affirms that it is only by the will of God that man has "dominion over all the earth," and that God alone is the Source of all creativeness.

Let it be clearly understood that giving up

melakhah is a positive spiritual act. Man's work in the week, and the illusion which it fosters, is as a veil which hides from him the true nature of his purpose in the world. Giving up *melakhah* means lifting the veil. So long as there is the slightest trace of *melakhah* in our life on Sabbath, the veil hangs in place. In the spiritual sphere, the smallest act can have as great an effect as the largest.

He who presumes to do even one single *melakhah* on this day thereby denies God as Creator and Master of the world. This is why desecration of the Sabbath by *melakhah* is equivalent in the eyes of the Torah to apostasy and idol-worship. On the other hand, when we see a Jewish boy or girl refrain from plucking a single flower on Sabbath, we see something that is a greater testimony to God than all the high-sounding words of poets and philosophers.

We can understand, therefore, why cessation from *melakhah* is the essential requirement of Sabbath observance.

3 *Classification by Purpose*

We have defined *melakhah* as any act which shows man's mastery of the world by the purposeful and constructive exercise of his intelligence and skill. This is the type of activity he must cease from on Sabbath, in order to acknowledge and do homage to his Creator.

The activities included in this definition are those which bring about significant changes in our environment for productive purposes. They comprise the whole range of human productive activities.

These are classified, for the purposes of the

Sabbath law, into thirty-nine categories, derived, as mentioned above, from the building of the desert Sanctuary. In this classification it is not the physical nature of the activity, but its object or purpose that is the deciding factor. This is fully in accord with the *melakhah*-concept developed above. It is above all the productive purpose which gives to the act its distinctive *melakhah*-character.

For example, one of these categories — (No. 2; see Table) — unites under one heading such varied activities as: sowing, planting, grafting, pruning and watering growing plants. All these have a common purpose, the promotion of plant growth — and they are therefore comprised in one *melakhah*-category. To take another example, the eleventh category (see Table) includes not only boiling, baking, frying, etc., but also industrial activities such as smelting iron, tempering steel, etc. The general principle in this case is: changing the physical or chemical state of a substance by means of heat.

AV AND TOLADAH

A representative *melakhah* is selected by the oral tradition in each case, to give its name to the category. This is the one actually used in the construction of the Sanctuary and is known as the *Av Melakhah*. In the first example cited above the *Av* is "Sowing" and this is the name of the category. In the other example "Baking" is the *Av*. Other members of the category, whose status as *melakhoth* is derived from the common purpose they share with the *Av*, are known as *Toladoth* (derivatives). For all practical

TABLE

of the

THIRTY-NINE CATEGORIES OF *MELAKHAH*

1. Ploughing
2. Sowing
3. Reaping
4. Sheaf-making
5. Threshing
6. Winnowing
7. Selecting
8. Sifting
9. Grinding
10. Kneading
11. Baking
12. Sheep-shearing
13. Bleaching
14. Combing raw materials
15. Dyeing
16. Spinning
17, 18, 19. Weaving operations
20. Separating into threads
21. Tying a knot
22. Untying a knot
23. Sewing
24. Tearing
25. Trapping or hunting
26. Slaughtering
27. Skinning
28. Tanning
29. Scraping pelts
30. Marking out
31. Cutting to shape
32. Writing
33. Erasing
34. Building
35. Demolishing
36. Kindling a fire
37. Extinguishing
38. The final hammer-blow (putting the finishing touch to a newly manufactured article)
39. Carrying from the private to the public domain (and vice versa)

purposes there is no difference between an *Av* and a *Toladah*. The Torah gives both of them equal status as *melakhoth*, and to do either of them intentionally is an equally grave desecration of the Sabbath.

The list given above (pp. 24-25) in connection with the Sanctuary is in fact identical with the list of the thirty-nine *Avoth Melakhoth*. In the light of the foregoing, each of these should be considered as a key word representing a whole group of activities directed towards a similar end.

In effect, the oral tradition gives us here a masterly summary of the *productive purposes* of mankind.

In Chapter Three an attempt will be made to define the common purpose underlying the various activities comprised in each category, and to give a selection of some of the *melakhoth* and rabbinical safeguards likely to be met with in practice.

Before undertaking this survey, however, we must now consider the special character of the last of these thirty-nine categories — the *melakhah* known as "Carrying."

4 *Special Significance of "Carrying"*

If we consider the categories listed on page 32, we see that almost all of them are clearly *productive* activities.

But what of "carrying"? It is by no means clear at first sight how this *melakhah* fits in with the general concept we have developed above. Indeed, "carrying" seems of all *melakhoth* least obviously a "work," even in the special sense in which we have learned to apply this term in the Sabbath laws. No essential change, no productive process seems to be involved. Perhaps for this reason, and because it needs so little preparation and skill, there is unfortunately hardly another law of the Torah that is so widely ignored as this. Yet, as we have seen, the *halakhah* places "carrying" unmistakably among the *Avoth Melakhoth*. It is the first *melakhah* to be treated of in the tractate *Shabbath*, and seven of the latter's twenty-four chapters are devoted to it.

PROPHETIC WARNING

Moreover, when the prophet Jeremiah was told to warn Israel that the future of the Jewish state depended on the way Sabbath was observed in it, "carrying" was given special prominence in this connection.

The passage reads as follows (Jeremiah 17:19-27):

Thus said the Lord unto me: Go and stand in the people's gate, whereby the kings of Judah come in and go out, and in all the gates of Jerusalem, and say unto them: Hear the word of the Lord, kings of Judah, and all Judah, and all the population of Jerusalem, who enter through these gates!

Thus says the Lord: Take heed for yourselves, and carry nothing on the Sabbath day, nor bring anything in by the gates of Jerusalem, neither carry out anything from your houses on the Sabbath day, neither do any other *melakhah*, but sanctify the Sabbath day as I commanded your fathers....And it shall come to pass, if you obey me implicitly,

says the Lord, to bring nothing in through the
gates of this city on the Sabbath day, to do no
melakhah thereon, then shall there enter in by
the gates of this city kings and princes sitting
upon the throne of David...and this city shall
be inhabited for ever. .... But if you will not
obey me in keeping the Sabbath day holy, and
not carrying anything when entering in at the
gates of Jerusalem on the Sabbath day; then I
will kindle a fire in its gates, and it shall
devour the palaces of Jerusalem, and it shall
not be quenched.

We have quoted this passage at length, firstly to show
the importance which the prophetic message ascribes
to "carrying" on Sabbath, but even more to remark on
the way this *melakhah* is singled out from all the
others and treated as if in a class by itself. We are
admonished "not to carry...nor to do any other
melakhah." This is something that needs explaining.

What feature is common to all the thirty-eight
categories of *melakhah* apart from "carrying"?
Without exception, as we have seen, they have to do
with the realm of nature. Their significance lies in the
changes they effect in natural objects, whether the
change is an actual, physical one, as in "reaping,"
"baking," "dyeing," "lighting a fire," etc., or whether
it consists in taking the object out of the realm of
nature and into the sphere of human power and
control, as in "sheaf-making" and "trapping."

SOCIAL ORGANIZATION

In the case of "carrying," however, neither of these

features is apparent. What is forbidden is to transfer
an object from the private to the public domain (and
vice versa), and from point to point in the public
domain. The exact definition of these terms will be
given in Chapter Three; we may note for the present
that the most usual form of this *melakhah* is
carrying between the house and the street, or from
house to house by way of the street. We are dealing
here with something which is clearly quite different
from the realm of nature. The house, the street, the
city — these belong to quite another sphere: the sphere
of *human society*.

If the other *melakhoth* show us man mastering and
controlling his natural environment, this one shows
him active in the social realm, carrying on the
intercourse of the community, circulating its material
goods between house and house, through street and
thoroughfare; not for trade only, but also for the
personal and social ends of everyday life. "Carrying"
is the characteristic *melakhah* by which man pursues
and attains his purposes in society. By ceasing from
each of the other *melakhoth*, we proclaim God as the
source of our power over nature. By ceasing from
"carrying" we acknowledge Him our Master in the
sphere of human society. This vast, complex world of
social organization — the world of house, street and
city — needs above all else the realization of God's
presence and God's purpose, the sanctification and
dedication which ceasing from *melakhah* expresses.
The community whose members refrain from
"carrying" on Sabbath places the seal of God upon its
social life.

Can we now perhaps understand the emphasis on "carrying" in Jeremiah's message to the state of Judah? This is in line with the message of all the prophets — that Israel can exist as a nation only if it knows itself to be the people of God. And what can better express this dedication of the community than ceasing from "carrying" on the Sabbath?

The picture is now complete. The concept of *melakhah* has been defined, and some of the ideas that may lie behind it have been sketched in. The most important, the vital task lies ahead. We have to see how the Torah wishes the sublime concept of Sabbath to be realized in practice, in detail, in our everyday lives.

3

Sabbath Observance in Practice

1 *Safeguarding the Sabbath*

We have seen the fundamental importance of the prohibition of *melakhah* on Sabbath. We have seen how even one *melakhah*-act on Sabbath strikes at the roots of the whole Torah and constitutes an arrogant denial of God and His mastery of the world.

We can now perhaps begin to understand the extreme gravity of this offence in the eyes of the Torah. We may now have an inkling of what lies behind such sentences as:

> Those who desecrate it shall die; anyone who does a *melakhah* on that day — that soul shall be cut off from the midst of his people. (Exodus 31:14)

Indeed, who could do such an act, knowing its full implications, unless he were already dead to all the spiritual aspirations of the Jewish people? It is the simple truth, which we have unfortunately witnessed so many times in latter years, that when the Sabbath goes out of the life of an individual, a family, or a community, their Jewishness is turned into a hollow mockery, soon to be discarded altogether by those who come after.

In matters of such seriousness, even unthinking transgressions must be guarded against. It is a very poor excuse, when fundamental questions of this nature are at stake, to say, "I wasn't thinking." Sabbath presents special dangers in this respect, since it concerns actions which we are in the habit of doing all the other six days of the week. Jews at all times, conscious of all that is at stake, have been determined not to be dragged down from their high purposes by habit and forgetfulness. They have therefore sought ways and means of protection against unintentional Sabbath-breaking.

The Sages have given practical effect to this endeavor by means of protective legislation, by the method known as "erecting a fence about the Law" (*seyag la-Torah*). A prohibition of this kind is called a *gezerah* (rabbinical decree), or, with special reference to the Sabbath laws, a *sh'vuth*.

In taking these measures, our Sages have acted with the full approval and authority of the Torah, which itself commands us to take effective precautions against the unwitting violation of its laws. Thus we find (Exodus 23:13):

"And concerning all that I have told you, you shall take measures to guard yourselves";

and again (Leviticus 18:30):

> "and you shall safeguard that which I have given into your charge."

Referring to enactments made by the Sages in pursuance of this divine command, the Torah says (Deuteronomy 17:10-11):

> "...and you shall carefully carry out all that they teach you....
> "You shall not turn aside from the word that they declare unto you, to the right hand, nor to the left."

These *gezeroth* are thus as binding upon every Jew as the Torah itself. Moreover, since in every case the reason for the decree lies in the frailty and forgetfulness of human nature, they must remain binding for as long as human nature remains unchanged.

Our Sages have restrained us in this way from doing on Sabbath many acts which, although not themselves *melakhoth*, could very easily lead to our doing *melakhoth*. This may be either:

(a) because they outwardly resemble *melakhoth*, and so can easily be confused with them; or

(b) because they are linked with *melakhoth* by habit in everyday life; or

(c) because the act itself normally involves or easily leads to a *melakhah* in practice.

Tearing up a piece of paper is an example of the first kind. It is not a *melakhah*—the constructive *melakhah*-character is lacking—but it bears enough outward resemblance to one (viz. cutting material to a required shape) for it to be prohibited as a precautionary measure. Our Sages, with their deep insight into the ways of the human mind, saw clearly that if we were allowed to do the one, we should the more easily be led into doing the other — the real *melakhah* — when the occasion arose.

Agreeing to buy an article is an example of the second kind. This is a situation habitually linked with a *melakhah* (viz. writing down a note of the agreement); it is therefore forbidden to enter into such an agreement, even verbally, on the Sabbath.

Climbing a tree is an example of the third type. It may easily lead to breaking a twig or tearing a leaf, either of which is, of course, an actual *melakhah*.

We shall henceforth refer to these three types of *gezerah* as the "resemblance" type, or type (a); the "habit" type, or (b); and the "conducive" type, or (c).

TOUCHSTONE

It has been proved countless times that if all these safeguards are conscientiously observed in practice as an integral part of the Sabbath law, the probability of actual desecration of the Sabbath is greatly lessened.

One's attitude to this safeguarding legislation is the touchstone of one's attitude to the entire institution of Sabbath — indeed to the divine Torah as a whole. The Jew who decides to take a *gezerah* lightly has already decided in his heart to treat lightly the Torah itself. He has forfeited the right to call himself an observant Jew.

It should be noted however that the Sages, in their great practical wisdom, restricted this type of legislation to the minimum necessary to avoid transgression of the actual Torah-laws. It is a halachic rule that "a protective measure is never enacted to safeguard another protective measure" (*Bava Metzia* 5b).

This reflects the realistic standpoint of the Torah itself, which, while insisting on the high standard demanded of the servant of God, nevertheless gives full weight to the practical necessities of everyday life.

2 *Practical Survey of the Melakhah Categories*

It must be emphasized that the notes which follow are intended only to give a general idea of the scope of this legislation, and of its systematic nature. They are by no means intended to be exhaustive. For the detailed knowledge essential to proper Sabbath observance there is only one course — *tsei u-lemad*: Go and learn! The laws must be studied under the guidance of a competent *talmid chakham*. If possible they should be learned at the source — Tractate *Shabbath* in the Talmud, and in the *Shulchan Arukh*, the standard compilation of the *halakhah* (Part I: *Orach Chayyim*, sections 242-416). The abridged version of this work, *Kitzur Shulchan Arukh*, is available in an English translation (Goldin, *Code of Jewish Law*, Hebrew Publishing Company), in which a selection of the laws relating to Sabbath will be found in Sections 72-94.

In the following brief survey a description of the type of activity included in each class will be followed by some of the *melakhoth* frequently met with in practice, and some of the relevant *gezeroth*.

CATEGORY 1: *Ploughing.* The class bearing this name comprises every activity by which the soil is made receptive for seed or plant; also the removal from the soil of anything that might hinder plant growth.

> *Melakhoth* include: digging; fertilizing the soil; removing stones from the soil; levelling the ground.
> *Gezeroth* include: strewing sand or ashes on the ground without levelling (an example of the "resemblance" type of *gezerah,* type (a); see above, page 40).
> Sweeping the floor with a hard broom (this is a *gezerah* of the "conducive" type — type (c); sweeping may lead to purposeful levelling, which is a *melakhah*).

This is the basic *melakhah* by which man prepares the earth to yield its produce. By desisting from it on Sabbath, in all its forms, we acknowledge that "the earth is the Lord's, and the fullness thereof."

CATEGORY 2: *Sowing.* This class comprises every activity by which the growth of plants is caused or promoted.

> *Melakhoth* include: placing seeds or fruit-stones in receptive soil (even in a flower-pot); pruning trees or bushes; watering the lawn, or plants or flowers; weeding.
> *Gezeroth* include: washing one's hands over growing plants or grass (c); renewing the water in a vase with cut flowers (a).

CATEGORY 3. *Reaping.* This class comprises every activity by which any growing plant is severed from its place of growth.

Melakhoth include: cutting or plucking flowers, grass, leaves, twigs, berries or fruits, from trees, bushes, etc., growing in the ground or in a flower-pot. This applies equally to mushrooms or other fungi, wherever they may be growing.

Gezeroth include: climbing a tree; leaning against a tree that moves under one's weight (c); horse-riding (because one might easily be led to break off a branch in passing, to use as a switch. This is a *gezerah* of the "habit" type — type (b).)

CATEGORY 4: *Sheaf-making.* This comprises every activity by which natural products are gathered together into a unit serving some useful purpose.

Melakhoth include: piling fruit into a heap for storage or sale.

Gezeroth include: making up a bouquet of flowers.

CATEGORY 5: *Threshing.* This comprises every activity by which a natural product (solid or liquid) is separated from its husk, or other natural container, or from the organic whole of which it is a part.

Melakhoth include: shelling nuts, peas, etc., for some purpose other than immediate consumption; pressing out the juice of fruits grown primarily for their juice: for example, grapes, olives; milking.

Gezeroth include: pressing out the juice of other fruits as a drink (a).

CATEGORIES 6-8: *Winnowing, Selecting, Sifting.* These comprise activities by which a mixture is improved by removing its less desirable parts.

Melakhoth include: sifting flour; straining liquids; skimming milk (except for immediate consumption of the cream). In a heap containing both good and wormy fruit, to make the heap more suitable for consumption by removing the bad. (This is the characteristic form of the *melakhah*, and in this form it is forbidden both by tool and by hand.)

Gezeroth include: In a heap containing a mixture of both good and wormy fruit, to take away the good, leaving the bad behind (a). This *gezerah* does not apply if the sorting is done by hand and for immediate consumption. Washing and peeling fruit and vegetables is similarly allowed for immediate consumption only.

NOTE: This *melakhuh* is not confined to foodstuffs only, but can apply to the sorting of a mixture or jumbled collection of any articles; for example, removing the broken ones from a pile of chairs.

These are essentially "sorting" *melakhoth* and represent a characteristic of human activity. By ceasing from them on the Sabbath in all their forms, we acknowledge the God-given nature of our human intellect. Great care should be taken when learning the details of this *halakhah*; it has not been possible to give more than a short outline in this brief summary.

CATEGORY 9: *Grinding.* Every activity by which a natural product or other substance is divided (by means of an appropriate instrument) into small particles, in order to make better use of it.

> *Melakhoth* include: milling or grinding corn, coffee or pepper; filing metals; pounding or crushing substances in a mortar.
>
> *Gezeroth* include: grating vegetables, cheese, etc. by means of a grater, etc; rubbing off clots of dried mud or clay from boots or clothes (a).
>
> It is further forbidden (by a *gezerah* of type (b) — the "habit" type): to prepare medicine, to take medicine, and to carry out any treatment, for the relief of discomfort or pain or slight ailments (since to do these things is habitually connected with the pounding of medicinal ingredients). This *gezerah* does not apply in cases of acute pain or actual illness. For further discussion of this question see section 4 of this chapter, page 64.

CATEGORY 10: *Kneading.* Activities by which small particles of a substance are combined by means of a liquid to form a dough or paste.

CATEGORY 11: *Baking.* Any activity which changes the state of a substance by means of heat, thereby improving it for consumption or use.

Melakhoth include: cooking in all its forms; heating water to over 104° Fahrenheit (40°C); adding ingredients to a boiling pot; stirring boiling food; pouring hot water onto tea-leaves or onto tea-essence, unless the latter has been kept hot on the "Sabbath-stove" (see below); melting down any solid (fat, wax, metals, etc.).

Gezeroth include: scalding dried or smoked foods; drying wood in an oven; adding cold milk to hot tea, unless the latter is at two removes from the fire (that is, the hot liquid must first be poured into a "second vessel," for example, a tea-pot, and from this into the tea-cup, to which milk may then be added) (a).

The "Sabbath Stove": The prohibition of cooking does not mean that we may eat only cold food on the Sabbath. On the contrary, no Sabbath is considered complete without some hot food.

How is this result achieved? — by the "Sabbath-Stove":

This means that one arranges the stove before Sabbath in such a way that the actual burners are covered, and it is also impossible to regulate the heat on Sabbath. (This is usually done by means of a sheet of tin placed on top of the cooker with the edges bent down to cover the controls.) Hot cooked food and an urn of hot water can then be placed on the stove before the commencement of Sabbath, with the heat adjusted to keep them hot during Sabbath until needed.

CATEGORY 12: *Sheep-shearing*. This comprises every activity which severs from the human or animal organism those parts which serve it as outer covering (integument).

Melakhoth include: cutting off or otherwise removing (by the appropriate means) hair, nails, wool, feathers, from a living organism.

Gezeroth include: pulling off nails, etc. by hand (a); combing the hair (c). (It is, however, permitted to brush the hair with a soft brush.)

CATEGORY 13: *Bleaching.* This class includes all activities by which garments or cloth are freed from dirt, dust or stains, or by which a gloss is imparted to them.

Melakhoth include: soaking clothes; rubbing; wringing; ironing; removing stains or mud by water or otherwise.

Gezeroth include: brushing clothes (a); handling wet washing (lest one come to wring it out) (b); hanging washing out to dry (c).

CATEGORY 14: *Combing raw materials.* Activities whose effect is to turn compact or entangled raw materials into separate strands or fibers.

Melakhoth include: combing raw wool; beating flax stalks to make fibers.

Gezeroth include: winding thread onto a bobbin or wool onto a card; disentangling woolen or other threads (a).

CATEGORY 15: *Dyeing.* Any activity which changes the

existing color (natural or artificial) of an object or substance.

Melakhoth include: applying paint or distemper to wall surfaces, etc.; applying dyestuffs to clothes; dissolving colors in water; mixing or blending colors; making color reaction tests in medicine.

Gezeroth include: adding coloring matter to food (unless required for immediate consumption) (a); wiping fruit-juice-stained hands on a white cloth (a). The application of "make-up," rouge, etc. is forbidden on Sabbath (a); cosmetics can, however, be obtained which last over the Sabbath.

CATEGORY 16: *Spinning.* Extraction of thread from raw material by drawing out, twisting or turning.

Melakhoth include: manufacture of plush and felt, and rope making.
Gezeroth include: re-twisting a thread which has become undone (a).

CATEGORIES 17, 18 and 19: *Weaving operations.* These three categories comprise the whole range of the weaving technique, from the insertion of thread into the loom to the removal of the finished article, as well as everything similar in effect.

Melakhoth include: knitting; crocheting; darning; embroidering; plaiting; basketwork.
Gezeroth include: plaiting hair (a).

CATEGORY 20. *Separating into threads.* The separation

of woven or other material into its constituent threads.

> *Melakhoth* include: unpicking any part of a knitted garment.
>
> *Gezeroth* include: removing tacking threads from a dress. Tearing off a piece of cotton-wool from the layer. Separating a twisted thread into strands (a).

CATEGORY 21: *Tying a knot.* Any activity which effects a lasting connection between two objects.

CATEGORY 22: *Untying a knot.* Undoing such a combination for some useful purpose.

> *Melakhoth* under the above two categories include: tying and untying a double knot between two ends of string, thread, laces, etc.
>
> *Gezeroth* include: knotting the end of a sewing thread (a). It is however allowed to tie and untie a bow, since this is intended merely as a temporary connection. For the same reason it is allowed to untie the string around food containers, if the contents are required for immediate consumption.

CATEGORY 23: *Sewing.* Any activity by which two materials (similar or dissimilar), or two surfaces, are permanently joined together by means of a third substance.

CATEGORY 24: *Tearing.* Undoing a combination of the sort referred to in Category 23 to facilitate re-joining.

Melakhoth under the last two categories include: sewing or undoing two stitches; sticking papers together with paste; stapling papers.

Gezeroth include: drawing a tape through hem-stitching. (Fastening by safety-pin is permitted, since this is only a temporary fastening.)

CATEGORY 25: *Trapping.* This class comprises every activity which so restricts the freedom of movement of an animal, bird, etc., that it comes under the control of a human being.

Melakhoth include: catching or trapping animals or insects by hand or in nets, traps, etc. (this does not however apply to domestic animals, unless control over them has been lost); closing a window to prevent the escape of a bird or butterfly which happened to fly in.

CATEGORY 26: *Slaughtering.* Any activity which terminates or shortens the life of any living thing, or causes loss of blood.

Melakhoth include: killing by any means (this applies equally to animal, bird, fish or insect); drawing blood for a positive purpose (for example, for a blood test).

CATEGORY 27: *Skinning* or *flaying.* Separating the skin of a dead animal from its flesh as a process of manufacture.

51

CATEGORY 28: *Tanning.* Activities by which raw materials are made more durable or otherwise more valuable for human use, by chemical or physical processing.

> *Melakhoth* include: all parts of the tanning process.
> *Gezeroth* include: oiling boots and shoes; salting and pickling fish, meat, etc. (a); soaking meat in water for "koshering" (a).

CATEGORY 29: *Scraping.* This includes every activity which removes roughness from the surface of a material by means of grinding, rubbing, polishing or otherwise.

> *Melakhoth* include: cleaning utensils with scouring powder or by machine; smoothening the surface of any substance; rubbing soap to make lather; application of ointment, face-cream, etc.; polishing boots and shoes.

CATEGORY 30: *Marking out.* This comprises the activities of marking or scoring lines on a surface, in preparation for cutting, or for writing, or for any other useful purpose.

CATEGORY 31: *Cutting to shape.* This comprises every activity by which the size or shape of an object is altered to one more suitable for human use, as a process of manufacture.

> *Melakhoth* include: cutting or tearing any material to a definite shape or pattern;

sharpening a pencil or toothpick; cutting out a newspaper paragraph. (Cutting up foodstuffs for immediate consumption is, however, permitted.)

CATEGORY 32: *Writing*. Comprises every activity by which significant signs are made in a durable manner on durable material.

> *Melakhoth* include: writing, drawing, painting, etc., by pencil, ink or other writing materials; embroidering patterns, letters or figures; making impressions on wax; typewriting; printing.
>
> *Gezeroth* include: making signs of a nondurable nature, e.g. drawing with the finger on a moist window-pane or tracing patterns in the sand (a); doing anything that is usually accompanied by writing, note-taking, etc., e.g. making appointments, buying or selling or agreeing to buy or sell; measuring and weighing; reading business correspondence; judicial acts; marriage, divorce, etc.; playing games for money (or promises of money!); betting (b).

CATEGORY 33: *Erasing*. Activities whose effect is the production of a clean surface for writing.

> *Melakhoth* include: any obliteration of writing whereby space is gained for new writing.
>
> *Gezeroth* include: (a) tearing through the writing on a food wrapper (unless the contents are urgently required).

CATEGORY 34: *Building.* This category comprises a wide range of activities connected with the concepts of structure and form; namely, all those which have as their purpose and effect:

(1) constructing, repairing, improving or making habitable or usable any structure or part of a structure;

(2) permanently joining together two or more things so as to make of them a usable whole, and

(3) permanently changing the configuration of any mass or substance for a useful purpose.

> *Melakhoth* include:
> (1) The whole range of building operations; levelling or smoothing roughness or unevenness in wall or floor; knocking a nail into a wall; hanging a door; inserting a window frame or window pane; erecting a tent.
> (2) Fixing together the haft and blade of an axe, or broom-handle and broom-end.
> (3) Digging a hole in the ground for storage; pressing substances into a mould, e.g. cheesemaking; clay modelling.
> *Gezeroth* include: opening an umbrella; opening out a folding screen; putting up a hood on a baby-stroller (a). (This *gezerah* does not apply if the tent-like structure, i.e. the hood, etc., was partially erected before Sabbath. Thus if the hood was extended a minimum of 4″ over the stroller before Sabbath, it is permitted to extend it fully on Sabbath.)

At first sight it may be difficult for us to see how, for example, opening an umbrella is similar to the *melakhah* as described. A little reflection, however, will reveal to us something of the depths of our Sages' formulation of *gezeroth*. In fact, in this example, besides the similarity in the activity (erection), there is also a similarity in the resulting structures (the umbrella open; the tent erect), and, further, an essential similarity of purpose (protection from the elements). We see how the Sages penetrated beyond ordinary appearances to the essentials beneath.

CATEGORY 35: *Demolishing.* Preparation of space for building operations by demolishing an existing building, or by undoing any of the operations comprised in the preceding category.

CATEGORY 36: *Kindling a fire.* Any activity which initiates or prolongs combustion (or similar light- and heat-producing processes).

> *Melakhoth* include: fire production by any means, including lighting one flame from another; poking the fire or otherwise increasing the flow of oxygen thereto; regulating a flame by turning it up or down; smoking a cigarette; producing an electric spark; starting or driving a motor-car; using the telephone; switching on electric light or any electrical apparatus.
>
> *Gezeroth* include: reading alone by lamplight (b); moving a lighted lamp or candle (c); traveling in a bus or car, even if driven by a non-Jew, is also forbidden (see section 3: *Work by a Non-Jew*). With reference to long-distance journeys, see chapter 4, section 8: *Travel on Sabbath* (page 75).

It is hoped that by now enough will have been said to leave no room for the foolish argument, so often heard in conversation about this *melakhah*, to the effect that "this was all very well in the olden days, when kindling a fire meant hard work—knocking heavy stones together and so on; but it cannot be meant to apply at the present day." This is so obviously based on ignorance of the Sabbath idea that it hardly needs refuting. (Incidentally, its use reveals the user to be as ignorant of the history of civilization as of the basic principles of the Sabbath. The method of kindling fire in use in Egypt at the time of the Exodus was based on the principle of the tinder-box and involved hardly more effort than striking a match.[1]) In reality, of course, this—and particularly in its modern forms—is one of the most fundamental and characteristic of all *melakhoth*, since it is the key to man's control of nature. It is fitting that many of the modern trappings of civilization, such as electric light, telephone, radio, etc., involving the closing of an electric circuit, should fall under this heading. By keeping us from this type of activity on Sabbath, the Torah wishes to dig out from us the very roots of *melakhah*.

CATEGORY 37: *Extinguishing a fire.* Any activity which terminates, shortens or slows down any of the above-named processes, for some productive purpose.

> *Melakhoth* include: putting out a candle to improve the wick.

---

1. Sir E. A. Wallis Budge, *The Dwellers on the Nile* (1926), p. 63.

Gezeroth include: extinguishing in any way for any purpose (a), e.g. turning out gas, switching off electric light. (This *gezerah* does not, of course, apply where the spread of fire might cause danger to life.)

CATEGORY 38: *The final hammer-blow.* This is a general category, comprising all activities which put the finishing touches to any manufactured article, according to the nature of the article and the usages of the trade concerned; also those which repair or improve any article.

Melakhoth include: imparting a glossy finish to an article; removing hanging threads from a new suit; inserting laces in new shoes; repairing a clock or any machine or instrument.

Gezeroth include: winding up or setting the hands of a watch or clock (a). Specialized activities requiring the use of complex or delicate instruments are in general forbidden, owing to the danger of inadvertently adjusting or repairing the instrument (b). For this reason it is forbidden to produce any musical sound on an instrument, or indeed to make any sound with an instrument designed for the purpose. Rowing and cycling are also forbidden under this heading (see also chapter 4, section 7: *"Sabbath" and "Weekday" Activities*).

CATEGORY 39: *Carrying.* This category comprises (1) removing an object, for any purpose, from an enclosed "private domain" (*reshuth ha-yachid*) to a "public domain" (*reshuth ha-rabbim*) or vice versa; and (2) moving any object a distance of four cubits (approximately 7 ft.) in a "public domain."

Whether a "domain" is termed "public" or "private" in this connection is not at all a question of ownership.

Private domain means, for this purpose, any enclosed space not less than four hand's-breadths (approximately 15 inches) square, bounded by walls not less than ten hand's-breadths (approximately 3 feet) high. The usual form of this "domain" is a house, garden, etc. The term also includes a depression or elevation of not less than the above dimensions in a public space; for example, a pit or a block of stone. A movable object of this size, for example, a box or a car, also constitutes a "private domain," if situated in a public space.

Public domain means a street, road or square, frequented by the public, unroofed, open at both ends, and having a width of not less than sixteen cubits (approximately 28 ft.).

Melakhoth under this heading include: carrying by hand, over the arm, over the shoulder, in the pockets, in a bag or case; throwing, pushing, pulling (in a container, on wheels, or otherwise), and handing objects from one "domain" to the other, or from point to point within the "public domain." There is no *melakhah* in carrying any object within the boundaries of a "private domain." If, however, the "private domain" exceeds a certain size, and in certain cases when it is in the occupation of two or more families, this is forbidden by the Sages as a *gezerah* (see below, under *Carmelith* (2), and under *Eruv Chatzeroth*).

As we have seen above (chapter 2, section 4), this is the characteristic activity of man in society, and by ceasing from it on the Sabbath we acknowledge God's sovereignty over the world of social relations. The circulation of material goods, whether for commercial, personal or social ends, is the life-blood of the community; and it is this which must be dedicated in its entirety to God on the Sabbath.

The *melakhah*-character of the activity appears only when the article is transported by the method normally employed to move such things from place to place during the week; i.e. by hand, in the pocket, in a case or in some similar manner. If the article is worn as part of one's personal attire, however, it is no longer an "object" which is being transported in the above sense. It belongs rather to the "person" of the wearer. Thus, carrying an overcoat over one's arm is a *melakhah*, but wearing one is not. Anything which is capable of being worn is — if worn — not within the compass of this *melakhah*. Thus a handkerchief may be worn as a scarf, or two tied together may be worn as a belt. It is also quite permissible to wear two overcoats one on top of the other, if required for any reason.[2] In none of these cases is there anything in the nature of a *melakhah*. On the other hand, to qualify,

2. *Shulchan Arukh, Orach Chayyim*, sec. 301, 36.

59

the clothing must be worn in the proper way; an overcoat draped over the shoulders would not meet this requirement.

Gezeroth include: wearing in the street such articles or ornaments which one might easily take off and so might inadvertently carry; for example, eyeglasses not permanently required (c).

A child may not be carried in the street on Sabbath; it is therefore advisable not to take little children too far from home. Children may also not be taken out in a stroller or carriage. In case of need, however, this may be done by a non-Jew.

In addition, several regulations have been made by our Sages in connection with this *melakhah*, some of which may be conveniently summarized under the following headings:

Carmelith (literally, "unfrequented place"[3]). This is the name given by our Sages to certain types of places which, while not having the special characteristics described above, are nevertheless liable to be confused with the "domains" of the Torah.
These include:
(1) A street less than 28 ft. wide, or lacking any of the other characteristics of a "public domain" — for example, a cul-de-sac.
(2) An enclosed space more than 50 yards

3. Rashi, *Shabbath*, 3b.

square, which is not the area attached to a house; for example, a park.

(3) Open country.

(4) Seas, rivers and shores.

It is forbidden as a *gezerah* (a) to carry from a *carmelith* to either a public or private domain and from either of these to a *carmelith*, and to carry a distance of 7 ft. within a *carmelith*.

M'kom P'tur — מקום פטור — (literally, "free place"). This is the name given to places which have the characteristics neither of the "domains" of the Torah nor of the *carmelith*, and concerning which no *gezerah* was made; for example, an enclosed space less than 15″ square in a public domain.

Eruv Chatzeroth — ערוב חצרות — (literally, "mixing" or "pooling of rights" in relation to occupied premises). If two or more Jewish families live in adjoining houses having direct communication with one another, or in separate dwellings in the same house, they are not allowed to carry from one dwelling to the other, nor in the parts used by all the tenants in common, unless an *eruv* has been made (*gezerah*, type a). This means that the various Jewish families combine, and pool their rights of possession, so that their dwellings are the joint property of them all, in which case the *gezerah* no longer applies. The symbol of this joint possession is the *eruv* — as a rule a loaf or matzoth deposited as their joint property in the custody of one of them. If there are also non-Jewish families in the building, one must first hire from them the right of way for the Sabbath. The same laws apply to an enclosed square, a cul-de-sac, or garden used by several householders in common.

We have already noted the deplorable ignorance and neglect among large sections of the Jewish public of these laws against carrying on Sabbath. Yet, as we have seen, they are of fundamental importance in the Sabbath scheme. Our Sages have decreed that the mitzvoth of *shofar* and *lulav* shall not be observed if the occasion for performing them falls on Sabbath. The only reason for this decree is: lest an over-enthusiastic Jew might forget it was Sabbath and inadvertently carry the *shofar* or the *lulav* in the street. Our great teachers considered the mere possibility of a desecration of the Sabbath by carrying to be of such consequence that they decreed the omission of these two important *mitzvoth* of the Torah rather than take that risk. Anyone who, for reasons of personal convenience, is inclined to treat the *melakhah* of "carrying" lightly is thus making a very grave mistake.

It is hoped that this survey of the *melakhah* categories has given the reader some little insight into the practical aspect of true Sabbath observance. With a little thought, it will be seen how each productive purpose, each individual *melakhah* which we have discussed, is a practical application of the funda-mental Sabbath-concept developed at length in chapter 2. It will be seen, too, how each *gezerah* is an expression of true Jewish *yir'ath shamayim* — of reverence for God and His commandments — and of the determination of the Jewish people not to let momentary weakness or forgetfulness rob them of their unique act of homage and service — cessation from *melakhah* on Sabbath.

3 *Work by a Non-Jew*

"See: God has given *you* the Sabbath..."
(Exodus 16:29).

It is thus the Jew who was blessed with — and who bears the responsibility of — the Sabbath. Nevertheless, in order to safeguard our observance of Sabbath, our Sages have decreed that we may not ask a non-Jew to do on Sabbath anything that we may not do ourselves. We are not allowed to benefit from a *melakhah* done for us by a non-Jew, even unasked.

Since the Sages enacted this measure as an additional protection for the Sabbath, they were able to make certain exceptions; for example:

(1) in case of illness (see below, section 4) or other emergency;
(2) lighting a fire in cold weather;
(3) to relieve an animal in pain;
(4) where the act is done for both non-Jews and Jews, and the former are in the majority.

It is further forbidden to engage a non-Jew before

Sabbath to carry out work on Sabbath, except under the following conditions:

(1) the non-Jew must work as an independent contractor, for a fixed sum for the job;
(2) the work must be done on the premises of the non-Jew;
(3) the non-Jew must not be bound to carry out the work on Sabbath.

4 *Illness on the Sabbath*

(1) *Minor Ailments*: A normally healthy person is not allowed to take medicine or receive medical attention, even from a non-Jew, in cases of slight indisposition or localized pain, such as heartburn, headache, toothache, constipation, etc. (This *gezerah* has already been referred to above under Category 9, page 46.)

(2) *Illness* (not involving danger to life): Where, however, the person has to go to bed, or the pain is so severe that the whole body is affected, or the temperature is above normal, the above *gezerah* does not apply. In such cases everything that is necessary for the patient may be done by a non-Jew, medicines may be taken and treatment received. If no non-Jew is available, a Jew may do things otherwise forbidden as *gezeroth*, but these should be done a little differently from usual, in order to keep in mind the exceptional circumstances.

It is permitted to take the patient's temperature.

(3) *Serious Illness*: Where there is any suspicion that the person's life may be in danger, it is not only

allowed, but a duty for every Jew himself to do whatever may be necessary to save the patient's life. "Desecrate on Sabbath, so that he may live to fulfill many Sabbaths" (*Yoma* 86a). The potential glorification of God's name which is inherent in every Jewish life outweighs the momentary desecration which saving that life may entail.

Further information on this subject is given in a booklet published by the Gateshead Jewish Religious Publications Committee, entitled *Care of Children on the Sabbath* (chapter 6).

5 *Resting the Animals*

In the Ten Commandments and elsewhere the Torah commands us to let our animals rest on Sabbath.

This means that we may not allow any animal of ours to do any *melakhah*, nor may we place any burden on it, apart from bridle and reins and anything needed for its protection.

To induce an animal to do a *melakhah* by leading it, driving it or calling it to a desired place is forbidden even when the animal is not our own (*mechamer*).

If, however, the animal wishes to do a *melakhah* for its own satisfaction, for example, to crop grass, we are of course not to prevent it; the Torah says, "so that your ox and your donkey may rest..." and depriving it of its satisfaction can hardly be called "rest" (*Mekhilta*, Exodus 23:12).

It is interesting to note here the essential difference between the prohibition of *melakhah* as applied to man and as applied to animals. For man, *issur melakhah* has the positive significance we have seen above; the prohibition flows from a higher concept than that of physical rest. In the case of the animal this is not so. The superficial argument against true Sabbath observance ("...after all, the Torah only wants me to enjoy myself, and if my enjoyment is a cigarette...?") can now be seen for exactly what it is worth. It expresses a desire to exchange the Sabbath of man for the Sabbath of the animal.

The Celebration of Sabbath

1 The Spirit of Menuchah

All the week we have worked. All the week we have lived in the illusion that power over the world is in our own hands. This has been a veil hiding from our eyes the truth that God is the source of all power.

On Sabbath we have ceased from work. We have given up all *melakhah*, down to the last detail. As a result, the veil has been lifted. Now we can glimpse in all its glory that truth which lies behind our purpose in the world.

This is a moment which must fill us with wonder and joy. It must awaken our hearts towards that spiritual contentment which is the secret of Sabbath rest.

This is *menuchah*—the blessing of Sabbath experienced to the full, in the ways the Torah has shown us.

2 *Welcoming the Sabbath*

The deep insight of the Torah into the human soul, and the genius of the Jewish people, have combined to ensure that this joy shall overflow into and transform our material surroundings. Sabbath, itself a great spiritual experience, is to be welcomed with wine and song and festive meal.

Throughout the thousands of years of its history Sabbath has always been a day of joy and gladness in the Jewish home. Its coming is an eagerly awaited event for which the family begins preparing days in advance. In fact, Sabbath casts its radiant glow over the whole week. The days themselves are named in Hebrew in relation to the Sabbath: "the first day to Sabbath," "the second day to Sabbath," etc. This is how the week looks to Jewish eyes:

SABBATH
Friday
Thursday
Wednesday
Tuesday
Monday
Sunday

Everything looks forward to Sabbath. Business and social arrangements are made in such a way that they will not interfere with the Sabbath. Little luxuries bought during the week are stored up for the Sabbath. When Friday comes the tempo increases. Every member of the household plays his part in the preparations. Above all, of course, it is the Jewish housewife who now comes into her own. It is her proud duty to ensure that the royal guest is received in a worthy manner. She must see that all the Sabbath food is prepared and cooked before Sabbath comes in, the "Sabbath-stove" is on, the table decked with fresh linen and sparkling silver, with wine and *challah* and the Sabbath lights. The whole family change into their Sabbath clothes and a festive air overhangs the house. The scene is set for Sabbath, the royal bride, to enter.

3 *Entry of the Sabbath*

Sabbath commences on Friday eighteen minutes before sunset, and lasts until nightfall (about one hour after sunset) on Saturday. The housewife should kindle the Sabbath lights before the Sabbath comes in. As soon as she has said the blessing over the lights (להדליק נר של שבת), Sabbath commences for her even if the official time has not yet arrived, and she may no longer do any *melakhah*.

For the other members of the family Sabbath commences at the official time, or at the moment Psalm 92 ("A Song for the Sabbath Day") is recited in the synagogue (whichever is the earlier).

4 *Sanctification (Kiddush)*

We are bidden to "remember the Sabbath day." This means that each Sabbath we are to utter words which will serve to impress on our minds the holiness of the day. This is the *kiddush* or "sanctification."

Although *kiddush* is made in the synagogue, it is everyone's duty to make *kiddush* at home, before the Sabbath meal, over a full glass of wine. In the absence of wine, *kiddush* may be said over the two *challoth* (Sabbath loaves). It is forbidden to eat on Sabbath before *kiddush* is made.

In the morning, before the first meal, another *kiddush* is made. If possible, this should also be made over wine, but other alcoholic liquor may be used.

5 *Sabbath Joy*

Three festive meals (שלוש סעודות) are to be enjoyed on the Sabbath: one in the evening and two during the day. These are accompanied by table-hymns (*zemiroth*) extolling the greatness of the day and the glory of God. It is a happy experience to see how the children revel in the lively tunes of these *zemiroth* and in the other eagerly awaited features of the traditional Sabbath meal.

All these things contribute to "the feeling of happiness and joy which the Jew experiences, after having worked diligently and uprightly all the week, when surrounded by wife and children, he lifts up the cup to God to greet the Sabbath. No lip has been able to utter nor pen to describe such happiness; it is the ineffable reward, the foretaste of the world to come, that remains forever a secret between God and the feeling Jewish heart." (Samson Raphael Hirsch)

6 *Farewell (Havdalah)*

We bid farewell to the Sabbath by making *havdalah* (literally, "division" — between the holy and the profane). This is best said over a full cup of wine, but other liquors, or beer, may be used. We take, too, sweet smelling spices, as if to compensate us for that fragrant breath of added spiritual life which only the Sabbath can give us, and which our Sages call *neshamah yetherah*, the "extra soul."

With a blessing for the gift of fire we mark our return to the world of production and the conquest of nature, with the lessons of the departing Sabbath in our hearts to fortify and direct us in the toil of the coming week.

Nothing may be eaten after Sabbath before *havdalah* is made. *Melakhoth* may however be done as soon as Sabbath is out, provided the *havdalah* is mentioned as prescribed in the fourth blessing of the *Shemone Esrey* of *Ma'ariv*. Alternatively, the words *Baruch hamavdil bein kodesh lechol* ("Blessed be He who separates the holy from the profane") may be said.

If otherwise impossible (for example, if no wine or other liquor was obtainable previously), *havdalah* may still be said on Sunday, Monday or Tuesday, for these three days still belong to the outgoing Sabbath. Wednesday would, however, be too late; because the next three days already belong to the Sabbath that is to come. Here, then, is another view of the week, as it looks to the Jew:

SABBATH

Friday	Sunday
Thursday	Monday
Wednesday	Tuesday

Thus Sabbath dominates the week, casting its radiance before and behind.

---

7 *"Sabbath" and "Weekday" Activities*

Sabbath has the power to release in us hidden springs of spiritual energy.

This spirit of Sabbath should express itself in all that we do on that day. "The way that you walk on Sabbath should not be the way you walk on a weekday; what you speak of on Sabbath should not be what you speak of on a weekday" (*Shabbath* 113). All our activities should be consonant with the dignity and restfulness of the Sabbath.

Thus we should not rush or hurry; nor pursue athletic sports. We should not use our time on Sabbath to do heavy jobs, for instance re-arranging the furniture in the house (although, as we have seen, no question of *melakhah* is involved). Again, we should not make any kind of preparation on Sabbath for a weekday, e.g. packing a suitcase or looking up a railway timetable for a journey to be undertaken after Sabbath. Similarly, we may not read business correspondence or engage in conversation on business matters.

MUKTSAH

Our sense of Sabbath as holy and unique must be carefully nurtured. The unnecessary handling of objects for which there is no use on Sabbath is not conducive to this end, and in addition is likely to lead to *melakhoth*.

This is the basis of the rabbinical measure known as *muktsah*. The effect of this is that we are not to handle on Sabbath any objects which, for one reason or another, were not intended by us for Sabbath use.

This may be because their nature makes them unfit for use on Sabbath (e.g. money); or because they are not normally used at all (e.g. pebbles); or because they simply were not there when Sabbath commenced (e.g. a new-laid egg). The meaning of *muktsah* is "set aside," or "excluded" — that is "excluded from our minds": that which it was not in our minds to use on Sabbath.

There are several different types of *muktsah*, of which the following may be considered the chief ones:

(a) Objects which, when Sabbath commenced, were inaccessible to use. Examples: fruit fallen from a tree on Sabbath; eggs laid on Sabbath.

(b) Objects which can never be brought into use on Sabbath without transgressing the Sabbath laws. Examples: animals; a lamp; money.

(c) Objects whose normal use is for a *melakhah* purpose. Example: tools. These may not be handled for their own sake, for example, to show them to a friend, but they may be used for a purpose not involving a *melakhah*. (For example, a hammer may be used to crack nuts.) They may also be moved if they are in one's way.

(d) Useless objects. Examples: broken crockery, pebbles, peelings, etc. (These may however be cleared away with a broom; see below.)

(e) Any object which, at the commencement of the Sabbath, served as a basis or support for a *muktsah* object, and was intended to continue this function throughout Sabbath. Example: a drawer containing money. (However, if the drawer contains other things besides money, this does not apply.)

It must be understood that what we are considering is a *gezerah* against *using* and *handling* certain objects. There is nothing against *muktsah* objects being moved indirectly, where necessary — i.e. so long as they are not moved directly by hand. For example, broken crockery may be cleared away by using a broom and dust-pan. Similarly one is allowed to have a *muktsah* object moved by a non-Jew.

If one takes up a *muktsah* object by mistake, one need not drop it on the spot, but may put it down in its proper place.

FREEDOM

The full effect of Sabbath is only felt when both body *and mind* are given over to the Sabbath ideal. "Six days shall you labor, and do all your work." This indicates, say our Sages (*Mekhilta*, Exodus 20:9) that when Sabbath enters we should feel as if all our work were completed, leaving our minds and bodies completely free.

In effect, this means that there should be no "hangover" from the world of the "weekday" to the world of Sabbath. The author personally knows people who, the moment they close the office door behind them on Friday afternoon, leave all worries and problems behind, and enter the Sabbath world as if such things no longer existed.

SABBATH ACTIVITIES

From this Sabbath world we have banished all traces

of *melakhah*, all "weekday" activities — even "weekday" thoughts and cares. For six days they have claimed all our interest and attention. What have we to put in their place?

The answer is: *menuchah*, and the interests and activities which flow from this.

For this *menuchah* is not merely a negative concept. It does not mean that Sabbath should be spent in the armchair. On the contrary, our release from weekday acts and attachments should set free in us latent spiritual forces. New interests and activities should arise to take the place of those set aside. For example, here the family comes into its own. The Sabbath meals should be focal points of family interest, when each member of the family should be encouraged to take an active part in the celebration of the day. Above all, the Sabbath provides opportunity and energy for that greatest of all spiritual pursuits — learning the Torah. Here the greatest and the least can meet. Here is wisdom, to be partaken of by each according to his powers and capabilities. Here is the voice of God, lovingly and faithfully transmitted by the Sages and scholars down the ages. A Sabbath on which this voice has not been heard is a Sabbath strangely misspent. The home where it is heard has found in Sabbath a heightened spiritual experience.

8 *Travel on the Sabbath*

The spirit of Sabbath is essentially restful. It is understandable therefore that our Sages should have imposed certain well-defined limits to journeys undertaken on Sabbath. Normally, one may not proceed more than 2,000 cubits (about three-quarters of a mile) outside the town or place in which one is spending Sabbath. This limit is known as the *t'chum shabbath*, the "Sabbath boundary." Vehicular travel is forbidden for other reasons (see pages 55, 57).

Long sea-journeys and the like may be commenced before Sabbath; the ship then becomes one's temporary domicile for the Sabbath.

9 *Children and the Sabbath*

Jewish parents have a religious duty to train their children in the way of the Torah from their very earliest years. This training must of course be by degrees, according to the capacity and intelligence of the child.

> "Train up a child in the way that suits him best; even when he grows old he will not depart from it." (Proverbs 22:6)

Certain rules have been laid down by our Sages as to the form this training should take at the various stages of the child's development.[1]

Stage 1. According to the wisdom of the Sages, the first stage in this training starts at birth. Even when the child cannot yet understand simple commands (i.e. from birth until about 1 or 1½ years) his parents should not induce him to do any *issur* (forbidden act) unnecessarily, whether it is forbidden directly by the Torah or by the Sages. (Thus one should not, except on medical advice, give him forbidden foods; neither

---

1. See *Orach Chayyim*, 343: *Mishnah Berurah* (3).

should one, for example, give him paper to tear up on Sabbath.) There is, however, no need to prevent him doing any such act if he initiates it himself. Training in positive commands is of course not yet applicable.

Stage 2. As soon as the child can understand simple commands, he should be restrained from doing any *issurim* unnecessarily, even when he initiates them himself. Training in positive acts is not yet applicable so long as the child has no appreciation of the nature of the acts involved. This stage may last from 1 (or 1½) to 3 (or 4) years old.

Stage 3. When the child begins to appreciate the nature of the various acts concerned, he may be progressively introduced to certain positive mitzvoth, and encouraged to participate in them according to his ability and intelligence. *Sh'ma Yisrael, berakhoth, tzitzith*, listening to *kiddush* and *havdalah*, eating in the *succah*, are among the first mitzvoth to which the child is usually introduced during the early part of this period. From the age of 5 or 6 onwards the child should receive practical training in all the mitzvoth applicable to him or her, so that in reaching religious maturity at 13 (or 12 in the case of a girl) the transition to full responsibility is effected without undue difficulty.

These rules apply to the mitzvoth in general, but they have special application to the Sabbath, because of its unique function in the training and dedication of the Jewish soul.

In the Jewish home the child sees everything centered around the Sabbath. All the "best things" are kept for Sabbath: the best clothes and best dishes, favorite cakes and candies, table hymns, *kiddush* and *havdalah*, his parents' company and attention; all the things in which the soul of the child delights are concentrated in these twenty-four hours. In this way Sabbath becomes the central point in the child's life. The restrictions which true Sabbath observance imposes are no longer felt as restrictions at all, but are accepted by the child as part and parcel of the glory of Sabbath.

(For a full treatment of problems connected with the care of children on Sabbath, see the booklet referred to above: *Care of Children on the Sabbath*, by Rabbi S. Wagschal: Gateshead Jewish Religious Publications, 30 Windermere Street, Gateshead 8, England.)

CHAPTER

5

Sabbath in the Modern World

1 *The Economics of Sabbath Observance*

A century and a half ago the so-called emancipation
of the Jews began. Until then Sabbath observance
had been almost universal among Jews. When they
stepped out of the Ghetto to take part in the economic
life outside, they gained wealth — some of them —
and, for a short while, political freedom. But they lost
the Sabbath, and with it the soul of our people. For
the ethical values that have become ingrained in the
Jewish character are largely due to the hallowing
influence of the Sabbath.

A similar situation arose fifty years ago, with the
mass emigration from the great centers of Jewish
population in Eastern Europe to England and
America. Now those centers themselves are
unfortunately no more and the Jewish masses of the
present day have become almost completely
estranged from the Sabbath. Observance in many

cases is limited to the meaningless lighting of candles in a darkened room.

The majority of these Jews feel the loss involved in giving up the Jewish Sabbath. But their plea is, "We cannot help ourselves; present-day economic conditions force us to work on Sabbath."

STANDING FIRM

But do they? There are thousands upon thousands of Jews at the present time who keep the Sabbath in spite of all economic difficulties. How do they manage it?

The truth is that present-day conditions are by no means exceptional in this respect. It has never been easy to keep the Sabbath.

Was it easy for the farmer in ancient times, dependent on his own labor and that of his household, when a day lost in the urgency of ploughing and harvest-time might mean the difference between sufficiency and starvation?

And was it easier for the medieval Jew, living in intolerable conditions and in complete insecurity, to call for a halt for twenty-four hours to his efforts to earn the meager pittance that was his livelihood?

Yet these Jews stood firm. The difference between their times and ours lies not in the external difficulties but in the will to fight where Sabbath is concerned — the determination to hold on to the Jewish Sabbath as to a life-line. Contact with a non-Jewish scale of values has robbed the Jews of their sense of Sabbath's supreme importance.

WILL TO CONQUER

After all, what decent man, whatever difficulties he had in earning a living, would accept a job as a paid spy to betray his country to the enemy? Only contempt would meet a man who pleaded that, economic conditions being what they were, he was forced to do this in order to earn a living. If only our Jewish people realized that the same applies to the Sabbath, which is the secret of our nation's existence, they would never agree to sacrifice the Sabbath for the sake of bread and butter, or as is more often the case, for the sake of increased comfort in life. A Jew would say, "Sabbath is the supreme value in life. It must not be touched. I must conquer or die"; and he would conquer.

For if the Jew is convinced that by breaking the Sabbath he is destroying what is most precious in himself, and breaking the link that binds him to God and the Jewish nation, and if he stands firm in this conviction, however great his difficulties may be, then in the end God will help him. The old promise of the Torah still holds good: "See that the Lord has given you the Sabbath; therefore he gives you on the sixth day the bread of two days." The present writer has seen so many examples of the fulfillment of this promise among Sabbath-observant Jews that he can only pity those who call this argument naive. No Jew has ever died of hunger on account of the Sabbath. But many Jews and even whole Jewish communities have disappeared from the stage of their people's history through breaking the Sabbath.

In the last resort Sabbath is the great measuring

rod of *bittachon*, the touchstone of our belief that a higher force rules and guides our lives.

He who knows that his livelihood depends not on men, nor on "nature," nor on "economic forces," but on God Himself, knows also that no real gain can come from work done in defiance of God on the Sabbath. How often can one see the imagined gains from such soul-destroying work cancelled by unexpected losses in other fields! And on the other hand, the person who stands firm and refuses to betray the Sabbath for the prospects of apparent monetary gain, will often find that the loss was after all only illusory.

RE-EDUCATION

The first step to be taken, therefore, if we wish to regain for the Jewish masses their lost Sabbath, is the re-education of public opinion to appreciate the Jewish Sabbath in its entirety, with all that it stands for.

Nevertheless there are solid economic factors which must be taken into account, for the Torah is on earth and not in heaven. It is based on the realities of everyday life. We must therefore do whatever we can to make Sabbath observance easier, and not rely on miracles. Planning, foresight and careful preparation are needed if an occupation is to be found in which Sabbath can be observed without undue difficulty.

CAREER GUIDANCE

This should be borne in mind in the first instance by parents when choosing a career for their child. When the difficulties have already arisen, it may be too late to do anything about it.

A "Sabbath Observance Employment Bureau" can do fine work in this connection. Its activities will, it is hoped, be extended to include vocational guidance, in conjunction with other Jewish bodies, with a view to giving parents and public the fullest details of careers and occupations in relation to Sabbath observance.

If only as much thought and determination were devoted to this problem as to other aspects of earning a living, many obstacles would disappear.

THE COMPLETE SABBATH

Yet one thing must not be forgotten. It is true that there can be no Sabbath without stopping work, in the economic sense. But it is also true that this alone does not make a Jewish Sabbath, as we have endeavored to show in the earlier chapters of this little book.

The *neshamah yetherah*, the "additional soul," which, as our Sages say, brings us that highest form of spiritual happiness created by the Sabbath, is bestowed only on a person *hameshamer Shabbath kehilkhathah* — who keeps it in strict accordance with the Torah. Cessation from work must be supplemented by cessation from *melakhah* if our Sabbath is to be what God intended.

In spite of all difficulties and of all indifference, the fight for the Jewish Sabbath must and will continue. The infinite blessing of this Sabbath must again become the possession of the Jewish masses. Until we achieve this aim any words about Jewish spiritual revival will be so much empty talk.

2 *Sabbath and the Jewish State*

In modern Israel the focus of the Sabbath question is quite different. For the individual, at any rate, the economic problem is no longer acute. If one wishes to have Sabbath-free employment there are ample opportunities at hand. Sabbath is the official rest day, and enterprises working on Sabbath are the exception rather than the rule.

This solves the problem only partially however. Just as an individual can have a rest day without having a real Sabbath, so can a state.

One can conceive Sabbath as a social necessity, or even as a time-honored national custom or tradition, and still miss the whole point of the Jewish Sabbath.

It must be kept as a God-ordained day, a day of cessation from *melakhah*, as defined by the Torah, undiminished by the demands of ignorance and undistorted by ideas gained from outside sources. Only then will it appear in its true form as the proclamation of God's presence in the midst of human endeavor and human society. Only then shall we clearly see its basic relevance to the problems of the age.

OUT OF THE RUT

It is well over three thousand years since the Sabbath was given to the Jewish nation, but no age has ever had more need of it than our own. Never has there been a generation with minds so obsessed as ours by *melakhah* — the control of nature by the power of the human intelligence. Our achievements in this sphere have driven us to a delusion of self-sufficiency; they have driven us away from God and the roots of our own being. Instead of giving us a stable world to live in, they have increased instability beyond all imagination and produced a mass of rootless, hopeless, fear-ridden humanity.

The Jewish Sabbath frees us from our bondage to *melakhah*, and points the way to sanity and to the recovery of the real roots of our existence. The Sabbath of the *halakhah* is a spark of hope in the dark vista of the modern world.

We, the Jewish nation, gave Sabbath to the world, preserved and cherished it throughout the millennia, for just such an age as this. Surely we ourselves should have ears for its saving message! After all, it is to us, in the first instance, that its message is addressed.

The Jewish state has a particular responsibility — and a unique opportunity — in this matter. It could, if it wishes, quell for once the raucous, insistent clamor of the modern world, and so let the voice of Sabbath be heard.

What does this voice say? It proclaims to the Jewish nation, and through it to the world, the necessity of serving a purpose higher than itself. It shows them the way out of the spiritual rut in which humanity is caught. It shows them that the labors of state and society, if they are to have value and meaning, must be devoted to only one end — the service of God.

ERA OF REDEMPTION

Seen in this light, the observance of the true Jewish Sabbath of the *halakhah* becomes a basic necessity if the Jewish state is to fulfill its high destiny.

Many problems of *halakhah* do of course arise in connection with Sabbath observance in a modern state. There are questions of the maintenance of power stations, essential services, international communications and internal and external security, to name only a few. This is not the place for a detailed examination of these questions. Once the fundamental importance of the Sabbath law to the Jewish nation and state is realized and accepted, however, all problems of this kind will be found to have a solution within the framework of true Sabbath observance.

Here again it is fitting to point out that if only the ingenuity, vigor and determination evinced in other spheres were devoted to this highest of all ends, many practical problems would cease to exist.

Modern science has posed many of these problems, and modern science can do much to solve them. For example, automatic milking machines, controlled by a time-switch, are now in use in some *kibbutzim*. Accumulators can be, and in some places in Israel in fact are, used to store during the week sufficient electricity to supply Sabbath needs. In some cases electronic devices — such as a simplified form of "electronic brain" — could be adapted to provide a solution. Set for example in a power station, these could be arranged before Sabbath to react to many different eventualities, so that no Jewish hand does a *melakhah* except when the Torah demands it, i.e. in case of danger to life. Thus science can contribute to that great glorification of God's name — the full observance of the Jewish Sabbath by the people and institutions of the Jewish state. Once it was accepted by the bulk of the Jewish nation, this unique act of homage and service would indeed be a herald of the Messianic era, when the nations will set aside their destructive ends, and unite in the service of the living God.

This is the meaning of a profound saying of our Sages (*Shabbath* 118b):

> If the whole of Jewry were to observe but two Sabbaths according to the *halakhah*, they would at once be redeemed.

INDEX

89

INDEX TO PASSAGES CITED